Maths Matters!

Decimals

Look out for these sections to help you learn more about each topic:

Remember…

This provides a summary of the key concept(s) on each two-page entry. Use it to revise what you have learnt.

Word check

These are new and important words that help you understand the ideas presented on each two-page entry.

All of the word check entries in this book are shown in the glossary on pages 45 to 48. The versions in the glossary are sometimes more extensive explanations.

Book link…

Although this book can be used on its own, other titles in the *Maths Matters!* set may provide more information on certain topics. This section tells you which other titles to refer to.

Place value

To make it easy for you to see exactly what we are doing, you will find coloured columns behind the numbers in all the examples on this and the following pages. This is what the colours mean:

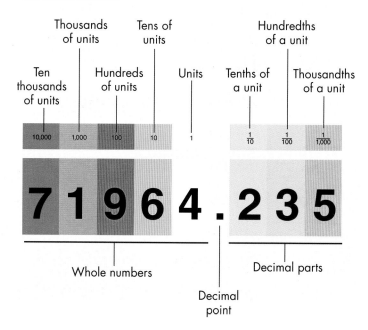

An *Atlantic Europe Publishing Book*

Series concept by *Brian Knapp and Duncan McCrae*
Text contributed by *Brian Knapp and Colin Bass*
Design and production by *Duncan McCrae*
Illustrations of characters by *Nicolas Debon*
Digital illustrations by *David Woodroffe*
Other illustrations by *Peter Bull Art Studio*
Editing by *Lorna Gilbert and Barbara Carragher*
Layout by *Duncan McCrae and Mark Palmer*
Reprographics by *Global Colour*
Printed and bound by *LEGO SpA, Italy*

Suggested cataloguing location
Decimals – *Maths Matters!* set, volume 6
    Decimal fractions – Juvenile literature
    Knapp, Brian and Bass, Colin
    513.5'5

ISBN 1 862140 26 X

This book is manufactured from sustainable managed forests. For every tree cut down at least one more is planted.

The 13 volumes in the *Maths Matters!* set are:

Contents

Introduction

37.9

234 mm → 23.4 cm → 0.234 m

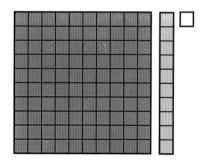

Decimal. This strange word comes from the Latin word *decima*, which means a tenth. A decimal system is therefore a set of rules that are based on tenths. This can apply to money (most modern money systems, or currencies, are based on 10's) or to measurement, as in the metric system.

But when people talk about decimals, they most often mean a number with a full stop or point in it. There are whole numbers to the left of the full stop, and parts of whole numbers to the right of the stop.

```
   0.56
 + 1.96
 ──────
   2.52
```

$$5 \overline{)5.6\,^{1}0}$$
$$1.12$$

$$0.07 = \frac{7}{100} \quad \text{(seven-hundredths)}$$

In fact, we meet this form of decimal all the time, because things rarely come in exact quantities. Few of the items we buy, for example, are bought in whole numbers.

But the really important thing to remember about working with decimals is that it means doing things in tens, whether it is money or measurement, or whether the numbers are bigger or smaller than one. And because ten is such an easy number to work with, you will find that decimals are surprisingly easy to understand whatever form they take.

3.141592654...

0.397

is bigger than

0.395

$$\frac{3}{4} = 0.75$$

Using a decimal point

Numbers with decimal parts must be written down very carefully. Otherwise you will not be able to see how big these numbers really are. The diagram below shows you how to write out a decimal number correctly. Notice that we have used coloured columns to make it easier to see the value of each number. An explanation of these columns is on page 2.

We separate the whole numbers from the parts by using a mathematical full stop, called a <u>decimal point</u>. It is shown by the "." symbol.

Units		Tenths of a unit	Hundredths of a unit
1	**.**	**2**	**3**

The number on the right is 1.23; that is, one whole unit, two tenths of a unit, and three hundredths of a unit. It is said as "One point two three".

← Whole numbers | Decimal point | Decimal parts →

This is the same number but with the columns taken away. The decimal point still marks the end of the whole numbers. Everything to the left of the decimal point is in whole numbers; everything to the right of it consists of parts of whole numbers.

1.23

Take a larger number such as 325.23.

Hundreds	Tens	Units		Tenths	Hundredths

3 2 5 . 2 3

Whole numbers ← → Parts of whole numbers

The further a number is to the left, the larger its value.

The further the number is to the right, the smaller its value.

We can see how it is made up of hundreds, tens, and units, and then (to the <u>right</u> of the decimal point) tenths and hundredths of units.

$+$ **3 0 0** Three hundreds

$+$ **2 0** Two tens

$+$ **5** Five units

$+$ **0 . 2** Two tenths

$+$ **0 . 0 3** Three hundredths

$=$ **3 2 5 . 2 3**

This is the number without the coloured columns. It is three hundred and twenty five point two three.

3 2 5 . 2 3

Remember... The decimal point tells us which are whole units and which are parts of units.

Word check
Decimal point: A dot written after the units when a number contains parts of a unit as well as whole numbers.

Decimals as shapes

If you are not sure what a decimal number is, then one way to understand it is to write out the problem in shapes, such as those shown below.

You might want to make your own shapes to work out other problems.

Let's begin with a whole number, in this case 237. It is made up of hundreds, tens and units.

Hundreds of units	Tens of units	Units
2	**3**	**7**

We could represent this number by shapes, such as these:

Two hundred
Hundreds

Thirty
Tens

Seven
Units

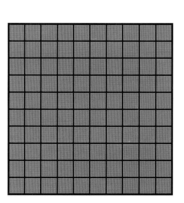

▲ **This is a shape for 100**.
It is sometimes called a <u>flat</u>.

▲ **This is a shape for 10**.
It is sometimes called a <u>long</u>.

▲ **This is a shape for 1**.
It is sometimes called a <u>unit</u>.

Each shape is ten times bigger than its neighbour to the right.

You can also use this system to represent a number containing a decimal point. Here we make the unit shape bigger to see that it, in turn, contains smaller shapes.

A unit is made up of ten tenths or a hundred hundredths. In this case a <u>long</u> then represents a tenth, and a unit represents a hundredth. See below how it is used to show 2.45.

Units	Tenths of a unit	Hundredths of a unit
2	. 4	5

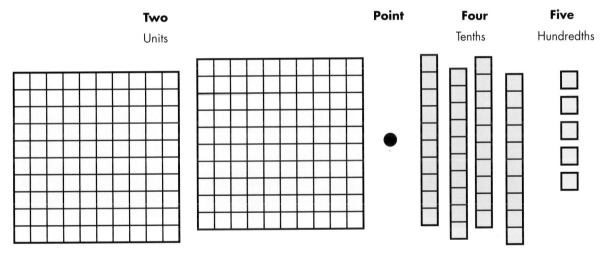

Two	**Point**	**Four**	**Five**
Units		Tenths	Hundredths

Remember... Whatever size your number, the neighbouring numbers are always ten times smaller on the right, and they are less than one if they are to the right of the decimal point.

Word check
Flat: A large square representing 100.
Long: A long shape representing 10.
Unit: A small square representing 1.

Decimals in money

All around the world people have realised that it is easier to use a money system in which numbers are multiples of ten.

Almost every currency in the world uses the decimal system to count in tens. The names for whole units and parts of a unit may be different, but they are all decimal currencies.

How we write a decimal currency depends on the unit we are using. For example, if we are using dollars, 23 cents is written down as $0.23, because 23 cents is less than a dollar. But if we are using cents, then 23 cents is expressed in whole numbers because the unit is the cent.

The same is true for other currencies, as you can see.

Dollars and cents

The dollar is the most widely used unit in the world. But a dollar is a large unit, and so there are also coins with a value of part of a dollar, for example 10 cents and 1 cent. There are 100 cents in a dollar.

The dollar is a decimal currency because cents, tens of cents and dollars (hundreds of cents) are all multiples of ten.

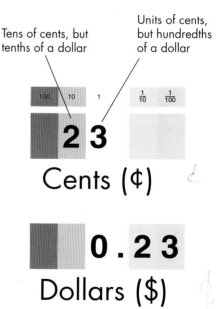

Tens of cents, but tenths of a dollar

Units of cents, but hundredths of a dollar

100   10   1 $\frac{1}{10}$ $\frac{1}{100}$

2 3
Cents (¢)

0.2 3
Dollars ($)

23 cents is two 10 cent coins and three 1 cent coins.

Pounds and pence

The pound is the unit of currency of the United Kingdom. There are coins with a value of part of a pound, for example, **10** pence and **1** pence. A pound is made up of **100** pence.

The pound is a decimal currency because there are pence, tens of pence and hundreds of pence.

Rupees and paisa

The rupee is the unit of currency of India. There are also coins with a value of part of a rupee, for example **10** paisa and **1** paisa. A rupee consists of **100** paisa.

Because there are paisa, tens of paisa and rupees (hundreds of paisa), the rupee is also a decimal currency.

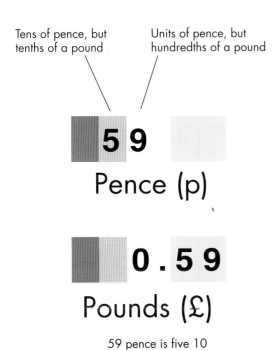

Tens of pence, but tenths of a pound

Units of pence, but hundredths of a pound

5 9
Pence (p)

0 . 5 9
Pounds (£)

59 pence is five 10 pence coins and nine 1 pence coins.

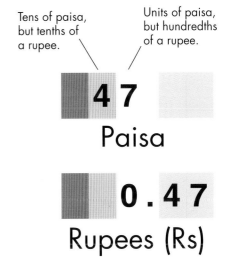

Tens of paisa, but tenths of a rupee.

Units of paisa, but hundredths of a rupee.

4 7
Paisa

0 . 4 7
Rupees (Rs)

47 paisa is four 10 paisa coins and seven 1 paisa coins.

Remember... The world works in decimal currencies, meaning that they are organised in multiples of ten.

Word check

Decimal number: A number that contains parts of units as well as whole units. The decimal point is used to separate the units from the parts of a unit.

Decimals in science

Science works with the metric system of metres, centimetres, and millimetres. It is fairly simple to change between measurements in millimetres, centimetres and metres by moving the numbers around the decimal point. These examples show how to do it.

In this example the height of a liquid in a flask was measured using a scale in millimetres. We found it was exactly 234 mm high.

In this case, all of the numbers would be to the left of the decimal point and so the decimal point is not used at all.

We could also have recorded the height in centimetres (centimetres are ten times as big as millimetres).

To change our measurement from millimetres to centimetres, we need to divide by 10: So, 234 ÷ 10 = 23.4 cm.

Notice that when we divide by 10, we move the numbers one place to the right.

Move the numbers
1 place right

We could also have recorded the height in metres (metres are 100 times as big as centimetres).

To change our measurement from centimetres to metres, we need to divide by 100: So, 23.4 ÷ 100 = 0.234 m

Notice that when we divide by 100, we move the numbers two places to the right.

Move the numbers
2 places right

Here is another example for you to look at. In this case, we read in metres first, then change to centimetres, and finally millimetres.

The height of the liquid in another flask has been read as 0.379 m.

0.379 m

There are **100** cm in a metre. If we wanted to express the number as centimetres, we would multiply it by **100**:

0.379 × 100 = 37.9 cm

Notice that when we multiply by **100**, we move the numbers two places to the left.

37.9 cm

Move the numbers
2 places left.

We could also express the height in millimetres. There are **10** millimetres in a centimetre. To change to millimetres, we multiply by **10**, moving the numbers one place to the left:

37.9 × 10 = 379 mm

379 mm

Move the numbers
1 place left.

Remember... When we <u>divide</u> a number by **10**, we move the numbers one place to the <u>right</u>. This is the same as moving the decimal point one place to the <u>left</u>.

When we <u>multiply</u> a number by **10**, we move the numbers one place to the <u>left</u>. This is the same as moving the decimal point one place to the <u>right</u>.

Word check

Decimal place: The digits used for parts of a unit, such as tenths and hundredths . For example, if a number is given to '2 decimal places', it means that there are digits in the tenths and hundredths columns.

Adding with decimals

To add with decimals, you first have to line up each number at the decimal point.

Once the decimal points have been lined up, adding with decimals becomes the same as ordinary addition.

For example, **345.23 + 467.39 = ?**

Put the decimal point in the answer in line with the other decimal points.

Decimal stretch

Jilly was working on a science project. She had discovered that a rubber band stretched **0.56** cm when she hung a **100** g weight from it, and **1.96** cm when she hung a **350** g weight from it.

Jilly then needed to add together the two measurements she had made to find out how far the rubber band would stretch if she hung a **450** g weight from it. For this she needed to add two decimal numbers as you can see here.

The answer was 2.52.

A zero (0) is written here to make it absolutely clear that the number is less than 1.

The numbers are lined up and then added together in the normal way.

Book link... This is an example of proportion. The stretching is proportional to the weight. See the book *Fractions* in the *Maths Matters!* set.

Making decimals whole numbers while you add

If you are still unsure about adding decimal numbers, you can turn them into whole numbers simply by making the decimal parts the same length, then dropping the decimal point. Add the whole numbers together and then put the decimal point back into the answer. Here is an example to show how it is done.

James wanted to measure the length of two pieces of wood he was working on. The first length of wood measured 3.56 m and the second length measured 4.76 m. Notice the decimal point is two numbers from the right in each case.

Step 1: As he did not feel sure about decimals yet, he decided to turn his decimals into whole numbers while he added.

Step 2: He lined up both numbers so the decimal points were above one another. Then he removed the decimal point.

In this way 3.56 became 356 and 4.76 became 476. He added 356 + 476 together. The total was 832.

Step 3: Finally, he had to convert his number back to a decimal number, so he placed the decimal point two numbers from the right in his answer, so that 832 became 8.32 m.

Remember... To add with decimals, either add normally, making sure you line up the numbers around the decimal point, or convert to whole numbers, add them together, and then convert back.

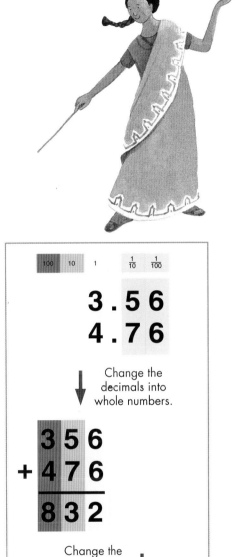

| 100 | 10 | 1 | $\frac{1}{10}$ | $\frac{1}{100}$ |

3 . 5 6
4 . 7 6

Change the decimals into whole numbers.

$$3\,5\,6$$
$$+\,4\,7\,6$$
$$8\,3\,2$$

Change the answer back into decimals by putting back the decimal point.

8 . 3 2

Adding decimals of different lengths

There is no fixed length for a decimal number. It may have one number to the right of the decimal point, two, three, or even more.

If you find that you have numbers of a different length to the right of the decimal point to add together, you need to follow this rule.

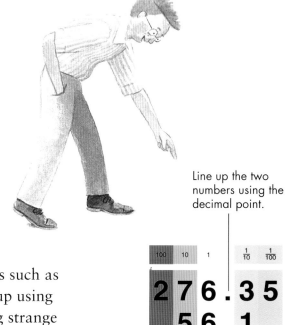

Line up the two numbers using the decimal point.

| 100 | 10 | 1 | $\frac{1}{10}$ | $\frac{1}{100}$ |

$$2\ 7\ 6\ .\ 3\ 5$$
$$5\ 6\ .\ 1$$

Suppose we have two unequal numbers such as 276.35 and 56.1. When we line them up using the decimal point, we notice something strange – they are not the same length!

But the numbers can still be added together. We simply need to put a 0 in the space as shown in the example:

$$2\ 7\ 6\ .\ 3\ 5$$
$$5\ 6\ .\ 1\ 0$$

Fill in a 0 here.

Then we can do the adding.

$$\begin{array}{r} 2\ 7\ 6\ .\ 3\ 5 \\ +\quad 5\ 6\ .\ 1\ 0 \\ \hline 3\ 3\ 2\ .\ 4\ 5 \end{array}$$

Suppose we have a whole number such as 357 and a decimal number such as 39.37. The whole number does not appear to be a decimal number. But we can convert it into a decimal number simply by adding a decimal point and a 0 after the whole number.

Notice that in this case we needed to add two 0's to make both numbers the same length as well as adding a decimal point.

Place a decimal point here.

Fill in a 0 here for every decimal place of the other number.

$$357.00$$
$$39.37$$

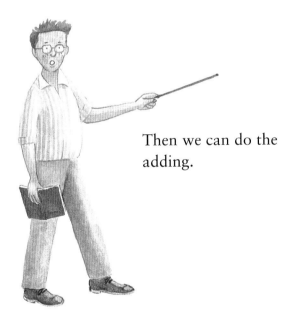

Then we can do the adding.

$$357.00$$
$$+\ \ 39.37$$
$$396.37$$

Remember... To add whole numbers and decimals, turn the whole number into a decimal by adding a decimal point and as many 0's as neccessary.

Subtracting decimals by exchanging

To subtract two numbers, first put the number you are subtracting below the one you are subtracting from, making sure the decimal points line up.

Then begin subtracting starting from the right.

The method of subtracting shown on these two pages is known as the 'exchanging' method.

Step 1: In this example we are subtracting the decimal 26.39 from the decimal 34.23. First line up the two numbers using the decimal points.

$$34.23 - 26.39 = ?$$

Both numbers line up around the decimal point.

10	1	$\frac{1}{10}$	$\frac{1}{100}$

$$3\ 4\ .\ 2\ 3$$
$$2\ 6\ .\ 3\ 9$$

Step 2: Start subtracting on the right (in this case, the hundredths column). Subtract the lower number from the upper number. Because 3 − 9 won't go, exchange one from the tenths column on the left and balance this out by adding 1 to the lower number of the tenths column as shown.

Now the subtraction is 13 − 9 = 4. Write down 4 in the hundredths column of the answer line.

Exchange 1 from the tenths column, making a total of 13 hundredths.

Balance this out by adding 1 to the lower number of the tenths column.

Step 3: Moving to the next column on the left (the tenths column), we find that 2 − 4 won't go. Again we need to exchange, but this time it is between the units and the tenths columns as shown. Now we are left with 12 − 4 = 8. Write down 8 in the tenths column.

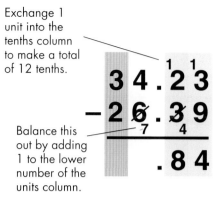

Exchange 1 unit into the tenths column to make a total of 12 tenths.

Balance this out by adding 1 to the lower number of the units column.

Step 4: Moving to the units column, we find that 4 − 7 won't go. Exchange between the tens and units columns as shown.

    We now have 14 − 7 = 7. Write down 7 in the units column.

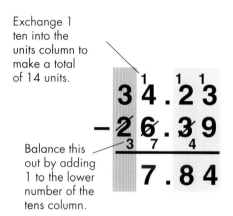

Exchange 1 ten into the units column to make a total of 14 units.

Balance this out by adding 1 to the lower number of the tens column.

Step 5: Moving to the tens column, we now have: 3 − 3 = 0. When a zero (0) is the first number, we normally leave it out, and so in this case we are left with an answer of 7.84.

The subtraction shown on these two pages is known as the 'exchanging' method.

Remember... Subtracting with decimals is no different from subtracting with whole numbers. You just have to remember to line up the numbers around the decimal points.

Word check

Exchanging: In subtracting, this is the method of taking 1 from the column to the left to use it as 10 at the top of your working column, and adding 1 at the bottom of the column to the left.

Note... You can subtract by the exchanging method shown on this page or by regrouping, as shown on page 20.

Book link... Find out more about exchanging and regrouping in the book *Subtracting* in the *Maths Matters!* set.

Subtracting decimals by regrouping

You may prefer to subtract using the 'regrouping' method, which is an alternative to the 'exchanging' method shown on pages 18 and 19.

In this case too you will still need to line up the numbers around the decimal points first. But the subtracting uses the following steps.

Both numbers line up around the decimal point.

Fill in a 0 here in the hundredths column.

$$
\begin{array}{ccc}
1 & \frac{1}{10} & \frac{1}{100} \\
\mathbf{2}.\mathbf{5} & \mathbf{0} \\
\mathbf{1}.\mathbf{7} & \mathbf{2}
\end{array}
$$

Step 1: Line up the two numbers using the decimal points. In this case we are subtracting 1.72 from 2.5.

If the numbers have an unequal number of decimals, add extra zeros to fill the columns. In this case a zero (0) has been added to the 2.5 to make it 2.50.

Step 2: Start subtracting on the right (the hundredths column). Take the lower number from the upper. Because 0 − 2 won't go, regroup one tenth as ten hundredths, reducing the tenths from 5 to 4 and increasing the hundredths by 10.

Now the subtraction is 10 − 2 = 8. Write down 8 in the answer line.

Regroup 1 tenth from the top of the tenths column to add 10 hundredths at the top of the hundredths column. Cross out the 0 and write a 10.

This leaves 4 tenths in the tenths column. Cross out the 5 and write a 4.

$$
\begin{array}{r}
\overset{4}{}\overset{10}{} \\
2.\cancel{5}\cancel{0} \\
-\ 1.72 \\
\hline
8
\end{array}
$$

Step 3: Now move to the next column on the left; the tenths column. Because we cannot take 7 from 4, we need to regroup 1 unit as 10 tenths, reduce the units to 1, and increase the tenths to 14.

Now we are left with the subtraction: $14 - 7 = 7$. Write down 7 in the tenths column of the answer line.

Regroup one of the 2 units as 10 tenths, and reduce it to 1. Make the top of the tenths column 14 tenths.

$$
\begin{array}{r}
\overset{1}{2}.\overset{14}{\cancel{5}}\,\overset{10}{\cancel{0}} \\
-\ 1.7\ 2 \\
\hline
.7\ 8
\end{array}
$$

Step 4: Moving left to the units column, $1 - 1 = 0$. When a zero (0) is the first number, we normally leave it out, but here we write down the 0 to make it clear that this decimal answer is less than 1. The answer to this subtraction is 0.78.

$$
\begin{array}{r}
\overset{1}{2}.\overset{14}{\cancel{5}}\,\overset{10}{\cancel{0}} \\
-\ 1.7\ 2 \\
\hline
0.7\ 8
\end{array}
$$

The subtraction shown on these two pages is known as 'regrouping' method.

Remember... You can subtract by regrouping or by exchanging, as shown on page 18.

Word check

Regrouping: In subtracting, this is the method of moving 1 from the top of the column to the left to use it as 10 at the top of your working column.

Book link... Find out more about exchanging and regrouping in the book *Subtracting* in the *Maths Matters!* set.

Multiplying a decimal by a whole number

If you have to multiply a decimal by a whole number, you can use this simple technique.

Here we want to multiply **6.5 × 7 = ?**

We are multiplying a decimal by a whole number. We can do this in a few steps:

Step 1: Count and remember how many places of decimals you have. In this case it is **1** place.

The decimal number 6.5 has been moved one place to the left to make the whole number 65.

Step 2: Convert the decimal number to a whole number.

Step 3: Multiply as you would for two whole numbers. That is: 7 × 65 = 455.

Step 4: Now change the answer from a whole number back into a decimal number by moving the number to the right the same number of places as in the original decimal number.

    In this case the number goes **1** place to the right. Notice the difference this makes to the value of the answer. It divides it by **10** from **455** to **45.5**.

Move the whole number 455 one place to the right, and insert the decimal point to turn it back to the decimal number 45.5.

Why does it work?

This method works because you really multiplied the decimal number by 10 when you moved the number one place to the left. Then you divided the answer by 10 to make it correct again when you moved the number back.

In step one on the opposite page we multiplied 6.5 by 10 to make the whole number 65.

$$6.5 \times 10 = 65$$

In step four on the opposite page we divided 455 by 10 to make the decimal 45.5 and give the answer to the original calculation.

$$455 \div 10 = 45.5$$

More practise

If we wanted to multiply 7 metres × 6.15 metres, you would have needed to move the number two places to the left to produce a whole number.

The number 6.15 is moved two places to the left.

The multiplication would become 7 × 615 = 4305.

A decimal point would need to be put into the answer two places back from the right-hand end. That makes it **43.05**. This is because 6.15 was multiplied by **100** when the number was moved, and **4305** was divided by **100** when the number was moved back.

The number is moved two places to the right.

Word check

Decimal place: The digits used for parts of a unit, such as tenths and hundredths. For example, if a number is given to '2 decimal places', it means that there are digits in the tenths and hundredths columns.

Remember… To replace the decimal point correctly when multiplying.

Multiplying with decimals

Two decimal numbers can be multiplied
together by first turning both of them
into whole numbers.

Measuring the weed killer

Sean and Kelly's dad wanted to buy
some weed killer for the lawn on his
way home from work. Unfortunately,
he had forgotten to measure the
lawn. He telephoned to ask the
children to measure it for him. The
lawn was shaped like a rectangle.
Dad asked the children to measure
the length and the width of the
lawn in metres, and then
multiply the two figures
together to find out the
total area of the lawn.

Sean measured the lawn very carefully. It was 7.1 m long and 6.2 m wide.

To multiply these numbers, the children first multiplied each number by 10. By doing this, they converted the decimal numbers to whole numbers.

Now they could multiply as normal. The answer was 4,402.

However, because they had multiplied each number by 10, and 10 × 10 = 100, the final answer was 100 times too big! So they had to <u>divide</u> by 100, which meant moving the number two places to the right. This made the correct answer 44.02.

4 4 . 0 2

Sean and Kelly's dad was very pleased when they told him their answer.

When he arrived at the shop, he discovered that the weed killer was sold in packs containing enough to treat either **30** square metres, or **50** square metres. Dad could therefore confidently buy the **50**-square-metre pack because he now knew that the **30**-square-metre pack would be too small.

30 < 44 < 50

Word check
<: The symbol for less than.

Remember... Multiplying your way out of trouble is fine. But you do have to put the decimal point back at the end!

Book link... Find out more about rectangles in *Shape*. Find out more about areas in *Size*, and find out more about multiplying big numbers in *Multiplying* in the *Maths Matters!* set.

More on multiplying with decimals

Here is an extension of the rule for remembering where to put the decimal point. It applies to all numbers.

To multiply two decimal numbers

Step 1: For the calculation 2.25 multiplied by 1.23, move the number to the left-hand end of both decimal numbers, turning them into whole numbers.

Step 2: Count and remember how many places you moved them. In both cases the numbers have been moved two places to the left, so the total number of places moved is 4.

2.25 × 1.23 = ?

In both cases, the decimal point is moved two places to the right to make the decimal numbers into whole numbers. These moves add up to total of 4 decimal places.

2.25 ⇨ 225

1.23 ⇨ 123

Step 3: Multiply the whole numbers together in the normal way.

Book link... Find out more on multiplication in the book *Multiplying* in the *Maths Matters!* set.

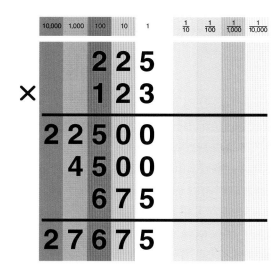

Step 4: Finally, change the answer from a whole number back into a decimal number by moving the number back from the left-hand end the total number of places counted in step 2.

2.7675

More about the lawn

Let's try using this rule on Sean and Kelly's lawn (see page 25). Suppose Kelly measured it as 7.1 m × 6.15 m. Notice that the two measurements do not have the same number of decimal places in them.

Change 7.1 into 71 and remember that the number has been moved 1 place.

Change 6.15 into 615 and remember that the number has been moved 2 places. This makes 3 places altogether.

Multiply 71 × 615 = 43,665

Move the number to the right 3 places. This is the same as placing a decimal point in the answer 3 decimal places back from the right-hand end. In this way Sean and Kelly find out that the lawn area measures 43.665 m².

Remember... You put the decimal point in the answer as many places from the right as the total decimal places in the numbers you multiplied.

6.15 × 7.1 = ?

In this case the decimal point is moved one place to the right to change the decimal number 7.1 into the whole number 71.

For the decimal number 6.15 the decimal point is moved two places to the right to produce the whole number 615.

The moves for these two decimal numbers add up to total of 3 decimal places.

$$7.1 \Rightarrow 71$$

$$6.15 \Rightarrow 615$$

$$
\begin{array}{r}
6\,1\,5 \\
\times \quad 7\,1 \\
\hline
6\,1\,5 \\
4\,3\,0\,5\,0 \\
\hline
4\,3\,6\,6\,5 \\
\end{array}
$$

$$43.665$$

Word check
m²: Metres squared.

Checking the decimal point

It is a good idea to check your maths work by a different method whenever you can.

We all make mistakes. It pays to find your own before anyone else does! It is especially useful when working with decimals to make sure that you have the decimal point in the right place.

Here is a quick method of checking that you have the right answer when multiplying.

The method

Step 1: Write down the numbers you want to multiply together using only the number furthest to the left. Write 0's in place of the others, and you have a simpler number to work with.

Step 2: Multiply these two simpler numbers in your head, taking care about the total number of 0's in your answer.

This should give you the approximate size of answer to the multiplication you are checking.

For example, suppose we want to multiply 52.34 by 14 using the method above.

$$52.34 \times 14 = ?$$

Step 1: 52.34 becomes 50 because the number furthest to the left is in the tens column.

14 becomes 10 because the left-hand number is in the tens column.

$$52.34 \Rightarrow 50$$
$$14 \Rightarrow 10$$

Step 2: $50 \times 10 = 500$

So when we multiply 52.34 by 14, we know our answer is around 500.

100	10	1
	5	0
×	1	0
5	0	0

This is the rough answer worked out using long multiplication.

When we work the sum out using long multiplication, the answer is exactly 732.76. But you can see that the rough check at least made sure that we knew the answer was in the hundreds rather than in the tens, thousands, and so on. And this check took only a few seconds.

10,000	1,000	100	10	1		$\frac{1}{10}$	$\frac{1}{100}$

$$5\ 2\ 3\ 4$$
$$\times\qquad\ \ 1\ 4$$

$$5\ 2\ 3\ 4\ 0$$
$$2\ 0\ 9\ 3\ 6$$

$$7\ 3\ 2\ 7\ 6$$

$$7\ 3\ 2\ .\ 7\ 6$$

This is the exact answer worked out using long multiplication of the whole numbers and then replacing the decimal point as shown on page 26.

Book link... Find out more on multiplication in the book *Multiplying* in the *Maths Matters!* set.

Another example, checking huge numbers also uses 'rounding'. For the calculation 5,678 × 87.65.

$$5{,}678 \times 87.65 = ?$$

Step 1: Round up 5,678 to 6,000 and 87.65 to 90.

$$5{,}678 \Rightarrow 6{,}000$$
$$87.65 \Rightarrow 90$$

Now the problem is 6,000 × 90.

$$6{,}000 \times 90$$

Split up the long numbers to make them shorter and therefore easier to multiply.
   You can now multiply the simple numbers in your head in any order you wish to make the approximate answer 540,000.

$$= 6 \times 9 \times 1{,}000 \times 10$$
$$= 54 \times 10{,}000$$
$$= 540{,}000$$

The correct answer is 497,676.7, and as you can see, 540,000 is near enough to make us sure that we are getting the decimal point in the right place.

Remember... Rough working out only takes a few seconds, and these few seconds are well spent if we can be sure that the decimal point is in the right place.

Word check
Rounding: Making a number shorter.

Book link... Find out more about rounding off numbers in the book *Grids and Graphs* in the *Maths Matters!* set and on page 36 of this book.
   Find easy ways of working out numbers in your head in the book *Mental Arithmetic* in the *Maths Matters!* set

Dividing a decimal by a whole number

When dividing a whole number into a decimal, just keep the decimal points lined up, and the decimal point in the answer will automatically be in the correct position.

You can use either short or long division.

Pizza sharing

José bought a pizza for $5.60 for himself and four friends. They divided it equally among the five of them and ate it. At the end of the meal the four friends wanted to pay José what they owed him.

The calculation was

5.60 ÷ 5 = ?

They did this by short division as follows:

Step 1: Divide 5 into the first digit. The answer is 1, remainder 0. Put in a decimal point.

$$5 \overline{)5.60}$$
$$1.??$$

Step 2: Divide 5 into the second digit, 6. The answer is 1 remainder 1. Carry the remainder right to make 10.

$$5 \overline{)5.6^{1}0}$$
$$1.1?$$

Step 3: Divide 5 into the third number, 10. The answer is 2, remainder 0.

$$5 \overline{)5.6^{1}0}$$
$$1.12$$

So each friend had to pay José $1.12.

Ben works it out

Ben wanted to compare accurately the thickness of a cassette box and a CD box. He stacked a sample of **15** cassettes along a table and measured the total length very carefully. It was **25.45** cm.

It was now easy for Ben to work out accurately how thick one of the cassette cases would be.

This is how Ben worked it out:

Step 1: Divide **15** into the first two digits. The answer is **1** with a remainder of **10**. Put in a decimal point. Bring down the next number, making **104**.

Step 2: Divide **15** into the remainder (**104**). The answer is **6** with a remainder of **14**. Bring down the next digit, **5** to make **145**.

Step 3: Divide **15** into the remainder, **145**. The answer is **9**, with a remainder of **10**.

Steps 4 onwards: Divide **15** into the remainder, and so on to get as many decimal places as you want.

The answer was 1.6966 centimetres.

Then he repeated the experiment with 15 CD boxes. You might like to find out how thick a CD box is using this method.

Remember... To divide whole numbers into decimals, you can use either short or long division.

$$\begin{array}{r} 1.6966 \\ 15\overline{\smash{)}25.45000} \\ 15 \\ \hline 104 \\ 90 \\ \hline 145 \\ 135 \\ \hline 100 \\ 90 \\ \hline 10 \text{ etc.} \end{array}$$

Word check

Digit: The numerals 1, 2, 3, 4, 5, 6, 7, 8, 9 or 0. Several may be used to stand for a larger number. They are called digits to make it clearer that they are only part of a complete number. So we might say, "The second digit is 4", meaning the second numeral from the left. Or we might say, "That is a two-digit number", meaning that it has two numerals in it, tens and units.

Changing fractions into decimals

Decimal numbers smaller than one can be expressed as fractions. Similarly, fractions can be expressed as decimals.

Here you can see how to change fractions into decimals.

You need only to divide the numerator (top number) by the denominator (bottom number).

Numerator

$$\frac{3}{4}$$

Denominator

If the numbers are easy, you might be able to do that in your head, and you will soon remember the common ones. For example ¾ (three-quarters) is exactly 0.75.

$$\frac{3}{4} = 0.75$$

If you cannot do the division in your head, write it down. You can use short or long division.

In many cases, after a few decimal places, the division will complete, and there will be no remainder. The fraction ¾ is such an example. By short division, ¾ works out to 0.75 exactly. Here is the working:

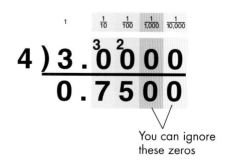

You can ignore these zeros

Here is another example. If we look at the fraction ¾

$$\frac{9}{4}$$

by short division, ¾ works out to 2.25 exactly. We worked it out like this...

$$4 \overline{)9.0^1 0^2 0\ 0}$$
$$2.2500$$

Common conversions

Here are some conversions that are often used in everyday life. Try to remember these.

¹⁄₁₀	(a tenth)	=	**0.1**
¹⁄₁₀₀	(a hundredth)	=	**0.01**
¹⁄₁₀₀₀	(a thousandth)	=	**0.001**
½	(a half)	=	**0.5**
¼	(a quarter)	=	**0.25**
¾	(three-quarters)	=	**0.75**

Sometimes, when we are converting a fraction to a decimal, the decimal number will not be completed but will carry on producing new digits for ever. Mathematicians call this a <u>recurring decimal</u>. Find out more about this on page 34.

It's common to see fractions and decimals together, as on this ruler.

This scale is divided into fractional lengths of ½, ¼, etc.

This scale is decimal; 0.1, 0.2 etc.

Remember... Every fraction can be converted into a decimal by dividing the top number by the bottom number.

Word Check

Denominator: The number written on the bottom of a fraction.

Numerator: The number written on the top of a fraction.

Recurring decimals

Sometimes when you try to convert a fraction to a decimal, the calculation cannot be completed, even if you carried on forever. Mathematicians call this a 'recurring decimal'.

One-third (⅓) is a very common fraction. It converts into a recurring decimal. Here is the working, done by long division.

3 divides into 10, 3 times with a remainder of 1. Bring down a 0... and 3 divides into 10, 3 times with a remainder of 1... And so on, for ever.

The answer is: 0.3333333333333333 33333333333333333333333333... for ever. Mathematicians say this as 'point three recurring'.

$$
\begin{array}{r}
0\,.\,3\,3\,3\,3\,3 \\
3\,)\,1\,.\,0\,0\,0\,0\,0 \\
\underline{9} \\
1\,0 \\
\underline{9} \\
1\,0 \\
\underline{9} \\
1\,0 \\
\underline{9} \\
1\,0 \\
\underline{9} \\
\text{etc}
\end{array}
$$

Not exactly...

Of course, 0.33 (using just the first two decimal places) is <u>not</u> exactly one-third.

The decimal number 0.33 is exactly the same as the fraction ³³/₁₀₀, and that is a little less than a third (⅓), as you can see by multiplying it by 3. So, 3 × 33 = 99.

The total is ⁹⁹/₁₀₀, which is a little less than 1.

$$0.33 = \frac{99}{100}$$

0.333 is <u>not</u> exactly one-third either.

The decimal number 0.333 is precisely the same as the fraction ³³³/₁₀₀₀, and that is also a little less than a third (⅓), as you can see by multiplying it by 3. So, 3 × 333 = 999.

The total is ⁹⁹⁹/₁₀₀₀, which is a little less than 1.

$$0.333 = \frac{999}{1000}$$

That can go on infinitely too. But if the decimal 0.33333333333333333333333333333 goes on for ever, it will be <u>exactly</u> one third.

Here is a story to help you see why that should be the case.

Eating ice cream for ever and ever...

Gill has a 1 kg (or 1000 g) tub of ice cream to share between nine children. They are very eager to see that it is shared equally.

She cannot measure exactly ⅑ th of a kilogram, so she measures ⅒ th (0.1 kg, or 100 g). The children each have a portion, and instead of eating the tenth portion herself, Gill keeps it for 'second helpings'.

Since this portion is 100 g, she divides it in the same way, keeping one portion back for 'third helpings' and giving each child 10 g or 0.01 kg.

Using this system, the children could go on eating smaller and smaller portions of ice cream for ever!

If Gill could go on dividing it in the same way until there was absolutely none left, each child would have had exactly ⅑ th of it.

This tells us the very strange result that:

0.1 + 0.01 + 0.001 + 0.0001 + and so on for ever...

$$= \frac{1}{9}$$ exactly.

Remember... A recurring decimal never ends.

Word Check

Recurring decimal: A decimal which shows new digits however many decimal places are used. There is always a repeating pattern, so although the digits go on for ever, we know what they are.

Rounding decimals

Calculators make division easy. But when you use them to divide, you can get a 'stampede' of numbers after the decimal point whether you are dividing whole numbers or decimal numbers. Here is how to avoid a 'stampede'.

Calculators do not have a brain to tell them what degree of accuracy to work towards. For example, when you divide 639 by 56 (639 ÷ 56) using a calculator, you get 11.41071429.

It is best to keep working with these long numbers until you reach the very end of your calculation. They help your calculator give you the most accurate answer.

But, as you probably only need a short final answer, perhaps with only a tenths digit and a hundredths digit, you have to 'chop off' the string of numbers the calculator produces. This is called rounding off.

How to use a calculator

Step 1: Enter 639
Step 2: Press division sign (/ or ÷)
Step 3: Enter 56
Step 4: Press equals sign (=)
(Answer reads 11.41071429)

Rounding up or down

Once you know what degree of accuracy you need, include one extra digit, and throw the rest away. In this example we have a figure showing 7.1421342 on our calculator, and we want only two decimal places (that is, to include tenths and hundreths).

The rule is this: if the extra digit is 0, 1, 2, 3, or 4, throw that away, too. But if it is 5, 6, 7, 8, 9, then increase the last digit by 1, and <u>then</u> throw the final digit away.

Below are the numbers you throw away.

$$1 \qquad \frac{1}{10} \quad \frac{1}{100}$$

If you want an answer that is accurate to 2 decimal places, look at the third decimal place. Since it is less than 5, we can throw it and all of the extra numbers away.

Take a look at another example: $\dfrac{6}{7} = 0.8571428$

Throw these away

We want an answer that is correct to 2 decimal places, so we throw away the fourth decimal and beyond.

$= 0.857\cancel{1428}$

This is the extra digit that you do not need for a 2-decimal-place answer.

But we see that the number in the third decimal place is 7.

$= 0.857$

Since the final number is 7, increase the last digit of the numbers we intend to keep by 1, making the 5 into a 6.

So we change the last digit in our answer to 6.

$= 0.86\cancel{7}$

$= 0.86$

Now we throw the 7 away.

This diagram shows why we increased the last digit. Clearly, 0.857 is closer to 0.86 than it is to 0.85, which is why it is rounded up to 0.86.

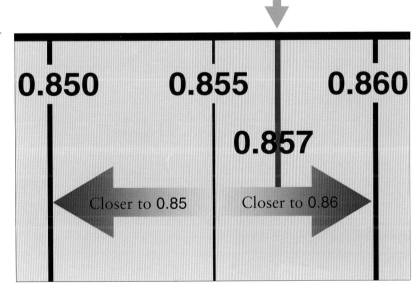

0.850   0.855   0.860

0.857

Closer to 0.85   Closer to 0.86

Remember... Decimal numbers are often rounded off. But remember to check the size of the digit just after the last one you want to keep to see if you need to round up or down.

Word check
Rounding: Making a number shorter.

Changing decimals into fractions

Turning decimals into fractions is not always so easy. Here are some hints.

Decimals with an end in sight

These are the simpler ones. To convert a decimal into a fraction, start by multiplying the decimal by 10, 100, or whatever number is needed to make the decimal into a whole number. Then simplify the fraction. For example:

0.4 can be made into a whole number if multiplied by 10. The calculation is:

$$0.4 = \frac{4}{10} \text{ (four-tenths)}$$

Now simplify the fraction by dividing the top and bottom numbers by 2.

$$= \frac{2}{5} \text{ (two-fifths)}$$
4 ÷ ?
10 ÷ 2

Other multiples of tenths are just as easy:

$$0.3 = \frac{3}{10} \text{ (three-tenths)}$$

$$0.07 = \frac{7}{100} \text{ (seven-hundredths)}$$

$$0.25 = \frac{25}{100} \text{ (twenty-five-hundredths)}$$
25 ÷ 25

$$= \frac{1}{4} \text{ (one-quarter)}$$
100 ÷ 25

Recurring decimals

These are the tricky ones. Mathematicians know how to convert every recurring decimal into an exact fraction, even horrid decimals like **1.696666...** which is the fraction $^{509}/_{300}$. Unfortunately, none of these methods is easy.

Pi, the impossible one!

There are some decimals which never end and never recur. However many decimal places are worked out, no repeating pattern can ever be found. There are lots of numbers like this, and a few of them are important.

The most famous is *Pi*. This is the number that you have to multiply the diameter of a circle by to find the circumference.

Throughout history mathematicians have devoted many years to calculating Pi to hundreds of decimal places. This was not because they needed to draw very accurate circles, but because they wanted to write Pi as an exact fraction, and so they hoped that the decimal would eventually recur. In 1882 it was proved that it never, ever would. So people now accept using a close approximate fraction of $^{22}/_7$.

3 . 1 4 1 5 9 2 6 5 4...

...is approximately equal to $\dfrac{22}{7}$

Book Link... Find out more about Pi in the book *Size* in the *Maths Matters!* set.

Word check

Pi: The number of times bigger the circumference of a circle is than the diameter. It is given a special name because it cannot be written down precisely as a fraction or as a decimal. It is approximately $^{22}/_7$ or 3.14159265....

Remember... To convert decimals to fractions, it is generally best to remember the conversions because there are not very many.

Dividing a decimal by a decimal

It is not difficult to divide a decimal by a decimal. You simply need to make the number you are dividing by into a whole number first.

Enough for all?

Sun's class was doing a science experiment by boiling salty water to find its temperature. His teacher mixed up 1.5 litres of salty water.

Brian was given a scoop holding 85 millilitres to make up to a 1-litre solution of salty water.

Claudia had to use two scoops of salty water before doing the same; Toto had to use three scoops; Elizabeth had to use four scoops, and Sun had to use five scoops.

Sun was worried that there would not be enough salty water left when it was his turn. He worked out that at least 15 scoops would be needed. He added up his friends' scoops like this: 1 + 2 + 3 + 4 + 5 = 15. To work out whether there would be enough salty water left, he needed to divide 1.5 litres by 85 millilitres. Since there are 1,000 millilitres in a litre, Sun worked out that 85 millilitres was equal to 0.085 litres.

85 millilitres = 0.085 litre

The problem that Sun needed to solve was therefore 1.5 divided by 0.085.

$$1.5 \div 0.085 = ?$$

Multiplying to remove the decimal point

One way around this difficult-looking problem is to turn the decimals into whole numbers by multiplying everything by 1,000. In this way 0.085 becomes 85 and 1.5 becomes 1,500. The division itself hasn't changed because all the numbers were multiplied by the same amount to express them as millilitres.

Now we can use long division. The answer is that there would be 17.6 scoops available.

Clearly this is more than the 15 needed. Sun need not have worried that there would not be enough for him!

Also…

In Sun's calculation the decimal point disappeared from the number he divided by (<u>the divisor</u>) as well as the number he divided into (<u>the dividend</u>). This does not always happen. The important thing is to remember to make the divisor into a whole number before you divide.

Book link… For more about long division see the book *Dividing* in the *Maths Matters!* set.

Remember… To divide decimal numbers easily, you need to multiply both divisor and dividend by the same number of 10's until the divisor is a whole number.

Word check
Dividend: The number you wish to divide into.
Divisor: The number you wish to divide by.
Quotient: The answer when you divide a dividend by a divisor.

Comparing decimals

It's handy to be able to compare decimal numbers quickly and easily. Here's how.

Everybody knows that 207 is bigger than 34. We know this because 207 has a 2 in the hundreds column while 34 has nothing in the hundreds column. This is true even though 34 has three tens and 207 doesn't have any.

It works the same way with decimals. A decimal with something in the tenths column must be bigger than another decimal with 0 in the tenths column.

Units	Tenths of a unit	Hundredths of a unit
0 .	**1**	**1**

This number contains tenths

is bigger than

0 .	**0**	**9**

This number contains only hundredths, there are no tenths.

Comparing significant figures

If the digits in the first decimal place are different, the one with the bigger digit is the bigger number. So, for example 0.8239 is bigger than 0.74589 as shown on the right.

0 . 8 2 3 9
is bigger than
0 . 7 4 5 8 9
or **0.8239 > 0.74589**

If the first digits are the same, we compare the second digits in the same way.

0 . 5 6 8
is bigger than
0 . 5 5 9
or **0.568 > 0.559**

If the first and second digits are the same, the one with the bigger third digit is the bigger number.

0 . 3 9 7
is bigger than
0 . 3 9 5
or **0.397 > 0.395**

And so on.

Check your measurements

When the decimals represent measurements, we need to be sure that the measurements can be compared (for example, all in metres, not some in metres and others in centimetres).

Here are some lengths arranged in decreasing size. They are all in metres for easy comparison. Any other unit for measuring length could also have been used, as long as it was used for all the examples.

	Metres
Height of this page	0.254
Width of this page	0.195
Height of a postage stamp	0.023
Width of a postage stamp	0.019
Thickness of this book's cover	0.003
Thickness of this paper	0.00012
Thickness of gold leaf	0.00004
Thickness of protective film	0.00002

Remember... To compare the size of decimals, line up the decimal points and compare the digits in each number, starting from the left. If they are equal, move to the next number on the right. If these digits are not the same, whichever is the bigger belongs to the bigger number.

Word check

>: The symbol for more than.

Significant figures: The numbers (reading from the left) that you need for your purpose. This is a way of describing how precise the number is. It is not affected by the position of the decimal point, which has more to do with the units being used.

What symbols mean

Here is a list of the common maths symbols together with an example of how they are used. You will find this list in each of the *Maths Matters!* books, so that you can turn to any book if you want to look up the meaning of a symbol.

— Between two numbers this symbol means 'subtract' or 'minus'. In front of one number it means the number is a minus number. In Latin *minus* means 'less'.

✛ The symbol for adding. We say it 'plus'. In Latin *plus* means 'more'.

✕ The symbol for multiplying. We say it 'multiplied by' or 'times'.

= The symbol for equals. We say it 'equals' or 'makes'. It comes from a Latin word meaning 'level' because weighing scales are level when the amounts on each side are equal.

$$(8 + 9 - 3) \times \frac{2}{5} = 5.6$$

( ) The symbols for brackets. You do everything inside the brackets first. Brackets always occur in pairs.

—, / and **÷** Three symbols for dividing. We say it 'divided by'. A pair of numbers above and below a / or — make a fraction, so ⅖ or $\frac{2}{5}$ is the fraction two-fifths.

■ This is a decimal point. It is a dot written after the units when a number contains parts of a unit as well as whole numbers. This is the decimal number five point six.

Glossary

Other symbols used in this book

< : The symbol for less than.

> : The symbol for more than.

m^2: Metres squared. A unit of area the size of a square measuring 1 metre each way.

This glossary contains the Word check items from earlier in the book along with many other terms commonly used in mathematics.

Adding: A quick way of counting.

Adding facts: The numbers produced by adding together numbers that we use a lot, such as $3 + 4 = 7$. These are facts we remember rather than work out each time.

Arc: Part of a circle. It is drawn using compasses.

Area: The size of the shape within a boundary. It is measured in square units by counting how many unit squares can be fitted into it.

Average: A number which gives you, in different ways, a single typical value for the data you have. Most people use the word average when they are actually talking about the mean.

Axes: The zero lines on a grid. The x-axis is across. The y-axis is up.

Back-to-Front Rule: When we add or multiply three or more numbers, we get the same answer whichever order we use.

Boundary: The line or curve separating the inside of the shape you are interested in from everything outside it.

Capacity: The maximum volume that a container can hold. It is measured in special units such as pints or litres.

Carrying: In adding or multiplying, when the working column total is bigger than 10, this is the method of adding the left digit at the bottom of the column on the left.

Chance: Something that occurs in an unpredictable way. You can forecast your chances in the long term, but you can never guarantee what will happen next.

Chart: A diagram used to show data from tables. There are many kinds of charts, including bar charts and pie charts. *See* Graph.

Circumference: The perimeter of a circle. In Latin *circum* means 'around' and '-ference' comes from a word meaning 'carrying'.

Continuous: A number scale which increases smoothly, without jumps or steps.

Co-ordinates: The pair of numbers that tells you the position of a point on a graph. They are usually enclosed with brackets.

Cubic unit: The same volume as is contained in a unit cube. It can be any shape.

Decimal number: A number that contains parts of units as well as whole units. The decimal point is used to separate the units from the parts of a unit.

Decimal place: The digits used for parts of a unit, such as tenths and hundredths. For example, if a number is given to '2 decimal places', it means that there are digits in the tenths and hundredths columns.

Decimal point: A dot written after the units when a number contains parts of a unit as well as whole numbers.

Degree: A small part of a complete turn. There are 360 degrees in a complete turn.

Denominator: The number written on the bottom of a fraction.

Diameter: The size of a circle measured straight across through its centre. In Greek, *dia* means 'through' and *metria* means 'measurement'.

Difference: The result when one number is subtracted from another.

Digit: The numerals 1, 2, 3, 4, 5, 6, 7, 8, 9 or 0. Several may be used to stand for a larger number. They are called digits to make it clear that they are only part of a complete number. So we might say, "The second digit is 4", meaning the second numeral from the left. Or we might say, "That is a two-digit number", meaning that it has two numerals in it, tens and units.

Discount: The amount of money the price is reduced by, often given as a percentage of the original price.

Dividend: The number you wish to divide into.

Dividing: A quick way of separating a number into many equal parts.

Dividing line: The line that separates the two number parts of a fraction. It is sometimes written horizontally, — and sometimes sloping, / . It is also called the division line. It is one of the signs mathematicians use for dividing. The other is ÷.

Divisor: The number you divide with.

Equals: The things on either side of an equals sign are the same.

Equation: A number sentence using the = symbol, telling us that two different ways of writing a number are the same. For example, $2 + 2 = 4$ and $9 - 5 = 4$.

Equivalent fractions: Fractions that have the same value.

Even number: A multiple of 2.

Exchanging: In subtracting, this is the method of taking 1 from the column to the left to use it as 10 at the top of your working column, and adding 1 at the bottom of the left column. *See* Regrouping.

Fact: A number produced by adding, subtracting, multiplying or dividing. It usually applies to small numbers that are learnt by heart, such as $7 \times 9 = 63$ or $8 + 9 = 17$.

Flat: A large square representing 100. It can also be made up of ten 'longs' put side by side.

Formula: A rule for calculating something. It is often an equation containing a letter or several letters.

Fraction: A special form of division using a numerator and denominator. The line between the two is called a dividing line.

Graph: A diagram with two axes on which points are plotted and then joined by lines. *See* Chart.

Grid: A pattern of lines that cross at right angles that is used to make it easier to set out your work.

Horizontal: Level and flat, like the surface of still water.

Improper fraction: A fraction whose numerator is bigger than its denominator.

Line: A continuous mark made on a surface. It may be straight or curved, and it can go on for ever in both directions.

Long: A long shape representing 10.

Long division: The way of writing down division by a number more than 10. The answer is written above the line, and the working is written in long columns down the page.

Lowest Common Multiple (LCM): The LCM of two (or more) numbers is the smallest number which is a multiple of them both (or all).

Mean: One form of average. It is calculated by dividing the total of the records in the data by the number of records in the data.

Median: One form of average. The middle number when the data are arranged in order of size.

Minus: Another word meaning 'subtract'.

Minus numbers: The numbers which fall below zero on a number line (scale). Minus numbers or zero cannot be used for counting, only for measuring things like temperature. Minus numbers are also called negative numbers.

Mixed number: A number made up of an ordinary fraction added to a whole number.

Mode: One form of average. The number or the group of numbers which occurs most often in the data.

Multiple: A number of objects which can be rearranged into several rows of equal length and longer than just one.

Multiplication facts: The numbers produced by multiplying together numbers we use a lot, such as $3 \times 4 = 12$. They are facts we remember rather than work out each time. Some people also refer to these multiplication facts as multiplication tables.

Numeral: A symbol standing for a number. (The modern numerals are 0, 1, 2, 3, 4, 5, 6, 7, 8, 9. Roman numerals are I, V, X, etc.)

Numerator: The number written on the top of a fraction.

Odd number: A number that cannot be divided by 2.

Odds: The ratio of expected losses to expected wins, used in betting.

One-digit number: A number between 1 and 9.

Operation: A mathematical word for one of the key methods: adding, subtracting, multiplying and dividing.

Ordered numbers: Numbers used for putting things in order, such as first, second, third, fourth, fifth and so on. Also called 'ordinal numbers'. *See* Unordered numbers.

Origin: The point where the axes of a graph cross.

Pair: Two things which match up in some way.

Parallel: Parallel lines are lines which will remain the same distance apart for ever.

Parallelogram: A four-sided shape in which opposite sides are parallel.

Per cent: A number followed by the % symbol means the number is divided by 100. It is a way of writing a fraction.

Perimeter: The size of the boundary of a flat object. It is the distance once around it. In Greek *peri* means 'around' and *metria* means 'measurement'.

Periphery: Another word for circumference.

Perpendicular: Two lines which meet or cross at right angles are called perpendicular.

Pi: The number of times bigger the circumference of a circle is than the diameter. It is given a special name because it cannot be written down precisely as a fraction or as a decimal. It is approximately $^{22}/_7$ or 3.14159265....

Place: The way we arrange numerals so that we know the value of a digit in a number.

Place value: The value of a digit due to its position in a number. For example, the value of a number placed to the left of a decimal point has a value in the units; a number placed two digits to the left of a decimal point has a value in the tens, and so on.

Plus numbers: The numbers which come above zero on a number line (scale). They are called this to separate them clearly from minus numbers. They are the same as counting numbers. Plus numbers are also called positive numbers.

Powers: Little symbols written above the line, like the 4 in 10^4. 10^4 is said 'ten to the fourth' and means 1 followed by 4 zeros, which is $10 \times 10 \times 10 \times 10$. Powers are sometimes called exponents or indices.

Prime factor: A prime number being used as a factor.

Prime number: A number which is not a multiple of anything (2, 3, 5, 7, 11, 13, 17, 19 etc., are prime numbers).

Product: The answer when two or more numbers are multiplied together.

Quotient: The answer when you divide a dividend by a divisor.

Radius: The distance from the centre of a circle to its boundary. It is half the diameter. In Latin *radius* means a 'ray' or 'wheel spoke'.

Ratio: A method of comparing different numbers by placing them on either side of a colon (:); for example 1:2. The numbers must be measured in the same units. The order of the numbers matters. A ratio is like a fraction.

Recurring decimal: A decimal which shows new digits however many decimal places are used. There is always a repeating pattern, so although the digits go on for ever, we know what they are.

Regrouping: In subtracting, this is the method of moving 1 from the top of the column to the left to use it as 10 at the top of your working column. *See* Exchanging.

Remainder: The number left over at the end of a division when the amount to be shared out equally could not be shared out completely.

Right angle: An angle which is exactly a quarter of a complete turn.

Rounding: Making a number shorter.

Row: Things placed side by side. In a table the entries which are in any line across the page.

Set: A collection of things we are interested in.

Short division: The way of writing down division by a number less than 10. The answer is written below the line, and the working is done in your head.

Significant figures: The numbers (reading from the left) that you need for your purpose. This is a way of describing how precise the number is. It is not affected by the position of the decimal point, which has more to do with the units being used.

Similar fractions: Fractions with the same denominator.

Single-digit number: A number between 0 and 9.

Slope: A surface or line which is not level. How much (or steeply) it goes up is measured by the ratio UP:ACROSS.

Sphere: A 3D shape made by spinning a circle around a diameter. It may be solid or just a surface.

Splitting-Up Rule: When two numbers are being multiplied, one of them can be split up into parts which are easier to multiply separately. The separate answers are then added together.

Square: A regular rectangle with all four sides the same length and four angles of equal size.

Square root: The number which, multiplied by itself, produces a square number.

Stepping stones: Easy numbers used to simplify finding your way through a calculation you are doing in your head.

Subtracting: A quick way of counting back to find out how many are left after you remove some.

Sum: The result of adding two or more numbers. *See* Total.

Symbol: A mark written on paper or something else to stand for a letter, a number or an idea of any kind.

Three-digit number: A number between 100 and 999.

Total: The answer to an adding problem. *See* Sum.

Triangle: A straight-sided 2D shape with only three corners.

Turn: Another word for angle. A quarter of a turn is 90°, a half turn is 180°, a full turn is 360°.

Turn-Around Rule: When we add or multiply the same two numbers, the answer is the same no matter which of the numbers comes first (but it does not hold for subtracting or dividing).

Two-digit number: A number between 10 and 99.

Unit: 1 of something. A small, square shape representing 1.

Units: A word used with measurement. For example, metric units.

Unordered numbers: Numbers used for counting when the order does not matter, such as one, two, three, four, five and so on. Also called 'cardinal numbers' or 'counting numbers'. *See* Ordered numbers.

Vertical: Upright, perpendicular to the horizontal.

Volume: The size of a 3D shape. It is measured in cubic units (such as cm^3 or in^3) by counting how many unit cubes can be fitted into it. *See* Capacity.

Whole number: A number containing only complete units, not parts of units (it does not contain decimals or fractions).

X-axis: The number line of a graph that goes across the page. *See* Axes.

Y-axis: The number line of a graph that goes up the page. *See* Axes.

Index